Anonymous

Rules of Discipline of Indiana Yearly Meeting of the Religious Society of Friends

Anonymous

Rules of Discipline of Indiana Yearly Meeting of the Religious Society of Friends

ISBN/EAN: 9783337169190

Printed in Europe, USA, Canada, Australia, Japan

Cover: Foto ©ninafisch / pixelio.de

More available books at **www.hansebooks.com**

Rules of Discipline

OF

Indiana Yearly Meeting

OF THE

Religious Society of Friends.

REVISED IN 1892.

RICHMOND, IND.:
M. CULLATON & CO., BOOK AND JOB PRINTERS.
1893.

INTRODUCTION.

Every association, whether it be religious, social, or civil, must establish its right to exist, before it can be accepted as a factor in promoting the welfare of the human family.

A declaration of principles is the first essential, and is the foundation for all future action.

Friends believe in the immediate revelation of the will of God to man, and that the natural man must be quickened and born unto eternal life before he can know the things of God. The Light and Power through which this new birth is experienced, is that which we are to mind, and this is the foundation of our beliefs.

Friends believe the declaration of the Apostle Paul to Timothy, to be true. "Every scripture inspired of God *is* also profitable for teaching, for reproof, for correction, for instruction which is in righteousness: that the man of God may be complete, furnished completely unto every good work." (II. Tim. 3-16.)

Therefore it is affectionately recommended that Friends, both old and young, make themselves familiar with the Holy Scriptures, frequently reading and meditating thereon, that the same Spirit which inspired the truths therein contained, may enlighten our understanding, and cause us to grow in spiritual strength and power; the older at proper seasons instructing the younger, that the same blessed experience of the work of regeneration, through the operation of the Spirit of truth, to which they clearly bear testimony, is to be witnessed now as in former ages, by all who attend to its manifestations. Thus, by the Divine blessing on our efforts, we may each and all be led into a firm belief in the Christian religion as set forth in the Scriptures, especially those parts which testify of the fullness of the Divinity in the humanity of

Jesus, the pre-eminent Son of God, and attain that end whereunto we labor—our soul's salvation.

A society which holds as a fundamental doctrine, *the immediate revelation of the Divine Will to the soul of every individual*, must accord the fullest liberty of conscience upon every question that does not conflict with that doctrine, or with the high standard of the Gospel.

Friends have always been seeking to know the Divine will, and this has kept them open to conviction, and the Light by which we are to walk, like the light of the sun, being fresh every morning, as we walk in its brightness (which is never obscured but by the mists which rise from our earthly natures), new presentations of the old truths will be disclosed, and methods of work must be formulated for the dissemination of these truths—methods that in former generations were not applicable to the conditions of society then prevailing, but which are essential to their furtherance as we understand them in their present acceptance. And as fresh needs must have fresh openings of Divine truth to meet and satisfy the hunger of the soul, it becomes a matter of the gravest concern that no barrier be maintained among us that obstructs the largest liberty of expression or of conscientious action that is consistent with the fundamental truths essential to the vitality of the society as a religious organization, so long as the spirit manifested gives evidence of a close walk with God.

With this large religious liberty, which we feel is necessary that the advancement of truth may be in no wise hindered, we record an earnest warning, that none shall misconstrue liberty to mean license, nor permit themselves to drift into luke-warmness, which is spiritual decay.

For the preservation of true Christian brotherhood, and the up-building of Christian influence, the society early adopted Rules of Discipline, in which it has recognized the equality of men and women in all matters of common interest which may claim the attention of the body.

[NOTE.—In the following pages, pronouns of the masculine gender include the feminine, and the singular number includes the plural in all consistent cases.]

ORIGIN OF THE SOCIETY OF FRIENDS.

The Religious Society of Friends was founded by George Fox, who began his ministry as an itinerant preacher in the year 1647. "He regarded the work in which he was engaged as in no wise the founding of a new sect or society, but, to use his own words, as '*the appearance of the Lord's everlasting truth, and breaking forth again in His eternal power in this our day and age in England.*' * * * As early as 1652 meetings of the followers of Fox, calling themselves at first the Children of Light, gathered together in various places in England, and were soon established in considerable numbers. The meetings at Bristol were often attended by from three to four thousand people. * * * The activity and zeal of the early Quakers (a name by which they are also known) were not confined to

England: they passed into Scotland and Ireland. Fox and others traveled to America and the West Indian Islands; one reached Jerusalem and testified against the superstition of the Monks; another visited Smyrna. the Morea, and the court of Mohammed IV. at Adrianople; others made their way to Rome; * * * two men passed into Austria and Hungary; and William Penn, George Fox and others preached Quakerism in Holland and Germany." [Enc. Brit., xx. 148.]

The first meetings of the followers were held in the year 1648. The first Yearly Meeting was held at Balby, in Yorkshire, England, in 1658. It was removed to London in 1661. These meetings, it appears, were meetings for worship only, as it was about the year 1666 when the first meetings for discipline were established.

A system of Discipline formed no part of the original compact of the society; there was not, indeed, to the human understanding, anything systematic in its foundation. It was an association of persons who were earnestly seeking after the saving knowledge of Divine truth. As soon as a few persons were joined together in the new bond of religious fellowship, they were prompted to admonish, encourage, and in spiritual as well as temporal matters, watch over and help one another in love. That the intent of the founders of the society was to make the discipline simply an instrument "for the civil and religious benefit of its members," and in no sense a "creed," is abundantly evident; any other conclusion would be not only in direct contradiction to the unbroken history of the society, but to the fundamental doctrine of the immediate revelation of the Holy Spirit.

The Yearly Meeting at London was not established, as it is now organized, until about the year 1678.

A Yearly Meeting was set up in Rhode Island for New England in 1661.

A "half-years meeting" seems to have been held at Oyster Bay, on Long Island, N. Y., as early as 1671.

The first Yearly Meeting held in New Jersey was at Burlington, 6th month 28th, 1681. In 1683, at a Yearly Meeting held at this place, it was proposed to establish a "General Yearly Meeting for all the Provinces, northward as far as New England and southward as far as Carolina," but the plan seems not to have met with favor.

In the same year a Yearly Meeting was held in Philadelphia, Pennsylvania, and in the years 1684 and 1685 the two meetings were held at Burlington and Philadelphia, but in the meeting at the latter place it was concluded that thereafter Friends in Pennsylvania and New Jersey should constitute but one Yearly Meeting, which should be held alternately at Burlington and Philadelphia.

In 1672 a Yearly Meeting was established and held alternately at Third Haven and West River, Maryland, which was changed to Baltimore in 1790.

The Yearly Meeting of Friends for Virginia was established 12th month 7th, 1702. It is believed that "general" religious meetings were held earlier, but there is no record of them.

One was held at Flushing, Long Island, in 1703, which was afterwards held at Westbury, Long Island, but in 1791 was removed to New York city.

A few Friends from Great Britain settled in Albemarle District, North Carolina, where, about the year 1708, a Yearly Meeting was established.

In 1809 a meeting was established in Canada, to be held twice a year, alternately at Yonge street and West Lake, known as Canada half-year meeting.

In a letter of George Fox "about the year 1689," he says the report to the Yearly Meeting at London gave the number of Yearly Meetings as twenty-six, but this undoubtedly included "Circular Meetings," which were for worship only. These meetings were held in Lancashire, Bristol, Wales, Aberdeen, Edinburgh, Colchester, Norwich, and other places

ORIGIN. 17

in Great Britain; also in Amsterdam, Dublin, Jamaica, Antigua, Barbadoes and Nevis.

The first meeting for worship west of the Allegheny mountains was held at Westland, a few miles west of Brownsville, Pennsylvania.

In 1812 Ohio Yearly Meeting was authorized, and it was organized in the following year at Mount Pleasant; it was composed of Friends residing west of the Allegheny mountains, belonging, with few exceptions, to Baltimore Yearly Meeting.

There are at the present time two religious societies in America calling themselves Friends. The one of which our Yearly Meeting is a part is composed of the seven Yearly Meetings of Baltimore, established in 1672; Philadelphia, in 1683; New York, in 1703; Ohio, in 1813; Indiana, in 1821; Genesee, in 1834; and Illinois, in 1875.

INDIANA YEARLY MEETING OF FRIENDS.

Indiana Yearly Meeting was authorized by Ohio Yearly Meeting, and established in 1821, being composed of Friends who resided in the States of Indiana, Illinois, and that part of Ohio west of the Scioto river. It now comprises Friends belonging to the Monthly Meetings which compose Whitewater and Miami Quarterly Meetings, and is held alternately at Richmond, Indiana, and Waynesville, Ohio (at Richmond in the odd and Waynesville in the even years), and meets on the Second-day next following the last First-day in the Ninth mo., at 10 o'clock A. M.

The Meeting for Ministers and Elders is held at 2 o'clock P. M. on the preceding Seventh-day.

Meetings for Public Worship are held at 10 o'clock A. M. on First and Fourth-days, and a meeting for young people at 3 P. M. on Firstday, unless otherwise ordered by the Yearly Meeting.

The design in the establishment of our annual meetings being the general oversight and care of the subordinate meetings in things pertaining to the welfare of the society, it is fervently desired that good order and harmony may be maintained in them. We know that love and unity, founded upon Christian principles, are promotive of truth and righteousness among ourselves, and we believe that when conspicuous in us, they will also have their influence for good upon those around us.

We therefore fervently desire that He who hath heretofore greatly blessed us will still animate us with a zealous concern that love may predominate individually, and unity prevail in every department of our religious body.

Therefore, let all our meetings be held as in the immediate presence of God, and may the reverence becoming the worship of Him be conspicuous in our assemblies.

Let the aged among us be examples of every Christian virtue, evincing by the calmness of their evening, that the labor of their day has not been lost.

Let the middle-aged not faint in the heat of the day, but with encouragement for the aged and the young, firmly support and exalt the precious principles and testimonies of Divine truth.

And may the beloved youth submit cheerfully to the guidance of their Heavenly Father, that, each standing in his allotted place, the harmony of the building may be preserved and we be truly a temple for the Lord, in which He may manifest the power of His love.

Previous to the opening of the Yearly Meeting the clerk should make a suitable arrangement of the business forwarded in the reports from the Quarterly Meetings.

Communications directed to the Yearly Meeting, except through the regular channel of correspondence, are to be examined by a nomination of Friends, who are to report whether the same are suitable to be read in the meeting. If not approved, no record of them should be made.

Two Friends of each sex are to be appointed as often as may be requisite, to forward epistles or other business to Yearly Meetings corresponding with this, who are to report annually.

MEMBERSHIP.

Applications for membership are to be made through the overseers to the Preparative Meeting; after that meeting is satisfied, they are to be forwarded to the Monthly Meeting, but where there is no Preparative, directly through the overseers to the Monthly Meeting, which is to appoint a committee to make inquiry as to the sincerity and propriety of the request, having regard to the importance of upholding our principles, and report their conclusion thereon. If this be favorable, and the meeting is satisfied, a minute should be made signifying the acceptance of such into membership, and one or two Friends appointed to inform the person thereof, and the clerk should forward the name to the Recorder.

When a request is made for membership the overseers should ascertain if the person making the request is acquainted with our Discipline, and if not, furnish him with a copy.

If overseers, after extending care, are satisfied it would not be desirable to present the application to the meeting, they shall, in the spirit of love, make known the obstruction to the applicant, and if he still desires to have his application presented to the meeting, it shall be forwarded thereto.

No past action shall be deemed a bar to restoration or acceptance into membership, if upon careful consideration a Monthly Meeting deems the person in proper condition for membership at the time of application.

Monthly Meetings should annually appoint a membership committee to exercise care in the following particulars: To extend special care to young members, and to endeavor to prevent any from growing luke-warm and drifting away; to manifest an interest in children and friendly persons, who, with proper encouragement, may become useful members of society; to supervise the record of membership, correspond with the absent, visit the luke-warm and those who from sickness or other cause are not able to attend meeting; to collect the accounts of births of members and report the same to the Recorder and to assist in making necessary changes and corrections of the register.

The committee may report for membership to the overseers, the names of persons who regularly attend our meetings and desire to become members, with such information as will enable the meeting to judge of the propriety of receiving them.

Persons who have been disowned for causes which are not now regarded as deviations from our order, may be visited by the membership committee, and if they desire and are thought worthy of membership, may be so reported to and received by the Monthly Meeting.

The committee should report every three months.

MINORS.

A child born while its parents are in membership has a birthright in the society and should be registered in the Monthly Meeting to which its mother belongs.

When one parent only is a member, the committee on membership shall collect (with consent of parents or guardian) the names of all such children under fifteen years of age, when it appears they are likely to be educated consistently with our Christian profession, and forward them to the Recorder for registration.

When both parents are deceased, any child (with consent of its guardian if there be one) may become a member by simple request of such child, at the discretion of the Monthly Meeting.

The blank on pages 26 and 27 is recommended as a proper form for registration.

RESIGNATIONS.

Should a member not under dealing wish to sever his connection with the society, he should make application to the Monthly Meeting, which, after inquiry as to his reason for so doing, may release him and inform him thereof.

MEMBERSHIP.

REGISTER OF

Consecutive Number.	Names of Members.	Parent's Number.	Residence.	Date of Birth.	When and to whom Married.

MEMBERSHIP.

MEMBERS.

Date and Received.	Date and to what Meeting sent.	Date of Disownment or Resignation.	Date of Death and Place of Burial.	Memoranda.

REMOVALS AND CERTIFICATES.

When a member removes from the limits of one Monthly Meeting to those of another, he should ask for a certificate of membership, directed to the Monthly Meeting nearest, or most convenient to his place of residence. Whether he make the request or not, his right should be seasonably transferred, to which end the membership committee should make inquiry, and if no obstruction appear, prepare a certificate, which, if united with by the meeting, should be forwarded as aforesaid.

If the certificate be for a minister, it should be so stated.

The meeting to which a certificate is directed should acknowledge its reception and acceptance, or give a reason for its return if not accepted. When accepted, a committee should be appointed to welcome the individual to his new associations.

Upon the removal of a member to another meeting, the register of names should be corrected, but his residence and post office address should be obtained and recorded.

Certificates of any who come among us professing to be Friends, if not seasonably produced, should be inquired for.

When a member has removed beyond the limits of his Monthly Meeting, and his residence cannot be ascertained, and he has been absent for a number of years without in any way claiming his right of membership, the Monthly Meeting, after the necessary care, shall be at liberty to discontinue it. If any such should return he may be re-instated.

CANCELLATION OF MEMBERSHIP.

The usefulness of the society demands that Monthly Meetings, after extending all right and proper care in the cases of those who are not in harmony with our principles and testimonies, and who persist in deviation to the hurtfulness of truth and the reproach of society, may have the power to cancel membership, though such action is to be earnestly considered, and done in that spirit of love which grieves that such action is found necessary.

STATISTICS OF MEMBERSHIP.

That the Yearly Meeting may be correctly informed of the number and location of its members, Recorders should make annual reports to their respective Monthly Meetings, in the Seventh month, stating the number of their members, and the additions and losses during the year. These reports should be forwarded through the Quarterlies to the Yearly Meeting.

The following form for statement is recommended:

STATISTICAL REPORT FOR 18....

....Monthly Meeting.

Males ....
Females ....

    Total Membership....................
Families.......................................
Parts of Families..............................

MEMBERSHIP.

GAINS FOR THE YEAR.

By Certificate..............................
By Birth ....
By Convincement...........................
By Correction of Enrollment............

  Total gains ....

LOSSES FOR THE YEAR.

By Certificates sent........................
By Death......................................
By Disownment.............................
By Resignation..............................
By Erasure....................................
By Correction of Enrollment............

  Total Loss...............................
Net Gain ....
Net Loss ....

REPRESENTATIVE COMMITTEE.

That the Yearly Meeting may be represented when not in session, it is directed that in the year 1893 and every three years thereafter, each Quarterly Meeting forward in its reports, the names of three suitable Friends of each sex, who, with fifteen of each sex appointed by the Yearly Meeting in the same years, are to constitute a Representative Committee, which is to hold meetings at such times and places as the Yearly Meeting may direct and upon its own adjournments. Special meetings may be held whenever eight of its members shall judge it necessary, all the members to be seasonably notified by its clerk, in person or by letter. The committee is to be governed by the following rules:

1. It shall keep minutes of its proceedings and report them to the Yearly Meeting.

2. Fifteen members shall constitute a quorum.

3. When a vacancy occurs, the clerk of the committee is to notify the meeting which appointed the missing member, so that the same meeting may fill the vacancy, and notify the committee (and in case the vacancy occurs in the Quarterly Meeting's appointment, it should notify the Yearly Meeting also) of the new appointment.

4. It is not to adopt any article of faith or discipline.

If a member of the committee is prevented from attending a meeting of that body, he should forward to its clerk a reason for his absence.

THE DUTIES of the Representative Committee are:

1. In general, to represent the Yearly Meeting and to act in its behalf in cases where the interest of our Society or of mankind seems to render it necessary.

2. To have the oversight and inspection of all manuscripts proposed to be printed or cir-

culated, relative to our religious principles or testimonies; and to advise or discourage the publication or circulation of them at discretion. It may publish or re-publish writings approved by it, and draw on the treasurer of the Yearly Meeting to defray the expense incurred in this or any other authorized service.

3. To inspect and ascertain titles to lands or other estates belonging to any of our Meetings when so requested; and to attend to the appropriation or disposition of charitable legacies and donations, or to give such advice respecting the same as may appear necessary.

4. To receive from the Quarterly Meetings such memorials concerning deceased Friends as shall be forwarded, inspect, correct if necessary, and if approved, forward them to the Yearly Meeting.

5. To receive from Quarterly Meetings accounts of such sufferings as may have been inflicted on members for faithfulness to our testimonies; to extend such advice and assistance to any so suffering as it may be able to render, and if necessary, apply to the govern-

ment or those in authority for proper relief, and for suitable legislation to prevent a recurrence of the trouble.

6. To correspond as occasion may require, with Representative Committees or similar bodies of other Yearly Meetings.

Visitors with minutes of unity, and members of other Representative Committees or equivalent bodies, may attend the sittings of this body, and other concerned Friends may do so with its consent.

Any member desiring to publish a book, pamphlet or paper upon the religious principles or profession of the Society, should lay the subject before the Representative Committee for its counsel and advice, or cause it to appear upon each copy printed, that it is done upon the responsibily of the writer alone, and not by permission or authority of the Society.

The Representative Committee and the Yearly Meeting alone, have the authority to publish official statements of our principles, and their publications should always have the imprint of their authority.

MEETINGS FOR WORSHIP.

Friends are admonished not to forget the importance of pure and spiritual worship. It is not enough that, after the example of our forefathers, we meet together in one place in outward silence; it is not enough that, with a commendable diligence, we attend all our religious meetings, unless also, like them, we wait in humble reverence for spiritual ability to worship God acceptably. Let all, therefore, seek for the Divine anointing, without which we can do no good thing, that we may experience the influence of the Holy Spirit to enlighten and quicken the soul to a true knowledge of its condition, and approaching the throne of grace under a renewed sense of our Heavenly Father's love, labor to forsake our errors, and to be clothed with the attributes of God.

This is the important purpose of our assembling together in silence; and though at times there may be among us but little vocal ministry, or even none, let not this produce any abatement of diligence in the duty. Vocal ministry in the life and power of the gospel is a great favor to the church, but the distinguishing excellence of the gospel is the immediate communication with our Heavenly Father, through the inward revelation of the spirit of Christ. Therefore, let the deportment of our members, while engaged in this solemn duty, be such as to demonstrate that they are in earnest in waiting upon and worshiping God in spirit, that serious, tenderhearted inquirers may be encouraged to come and partake in our assemblies of that inward, spiritual refreshment and consolation which the Lord is graciously pleased to impart to the souls of such as are humbled in His sight, and approach His presence with reverence and love.

It is desired that Friends be punctual and

constant in the attendance of our meetings, and that they conduct themselves in a manner becoming our high profession, and that they endeavor to keep their children, and such members as are under their care, to a regular, seasonable and orderly attendance of them also, instructing them to wait in stillness upon the Lord, that they may receive His spiritual favor, and by its tendering influence be engaged to walk worthy of such grace, and thereby become dedicated witnesses for Him among men.

As the occasion of our religious meetings is solemn, care should be taken to guard against everything tending to disorder or interruption. None are to oppose, in a religious meeting, a Friend when publicly speaking, whether he be a recommended minister or not, whilst in unity as a member, nor show any dislike; but if any have objections to what is delivered, he should speak to the individual privately.

If any continue to neglect the attendance of our religious meetings, or persist in disturbing them when present, their cases should claim the attention of the Monthly Meeting.

MEETINGS FOR DISCIPLINE.

Meetings for Discipline are instituted for the civil and religious benefit of the Society, and are designed to carry its purposes into effect.

They may be held in joint session of men and women, or with the sexes separate, and if separate, either department may originate measures that, in its judgment, the welfare of society or the common cause may seem to demand; but the final ratification thereof must be by concurrent action. Members are urged to be diligent in the attendance of these meetings, and cautioned to observe Christian dignity and forbearance in the consideration of all subjects claiming their attention.

The young are especially encouraged to attend and take part in the proceedings.

The meetings for discipline are:

First. The Yearly Meeting, from which all disciplinary authority emanates, being an annual assemblage of the members of its subordinate meetings. It is composed of two or more Quarterly Meetings.

Second. Quarterly Meetings, which, being subordinate to the Yearly Meeting, are to report to it annually in writing, and appoint four or more Friends severally to represent them therein. They are held once in three months, and are composed of two or more Monthly Meetings.

Third. Monthly Meetings, which are subordinate to the Quarterly Meetings, to which they are respectively to report in writing, and to appoint two or more Friends to attend as representatives thereto and report the exercises therein to their respective Monthly Meetings. They are composed of one or more Preparative Meetings, or meetings for worship.

Quarterly Meetings may set up Executive Meetings, with the same powers and duties as Monthly Meetings, to be held once in three months. These may hold extra sessions when necessary upon the call of the Overseers, who shall give notice thereof at the close of a previous meeting for worship. In this discipline the term "Monthly Meeting" shall include "Executive Meeting" in all consistent cases.

Fourth. Preparative meetings, which are established by Monthly Meetings, with the approbation of the Quarterly Meeting, and are composed of one or more meetings for worship. They are subordinate to the Monthly Meetings, from which they derive their existence, and to which they are to forward all subjects that require the attention thereof, and keep minutes of the same. Any Preparative Meeting whose members compose a Monthly Meeting may be discontinued.

Where a few members are situated remote

from any Meeting of Friends, they may, upon request, be granted by the Monthly Meeting to which they belong, the privilege of holding meetings for worship at such stated times as they may desire. Such meetings shall be under the care of the Monthly Meeting, which is to report the condition thereof to the Quarterly Meeting.

In making appointments, care should be taken to select those who are qualified for the service. No absent member should be appointed, unless the meeting desires such to serve upon the Representative Committee, or Committee on Philanthropic Labor, in which case they should be notified by the Clerk. Those who have accepted appointments should be punctual and diligent in attending thereto.

If a representative to a superior meeting be prevented from attending it, he should forward a reason for his absence; but if he fail to do this, the superior meeting should instruct the meeting that appointed him to furnish it with a reason for his non-attendance.

MEETINGS FOR DISCIPLINE. 43

When present, a representative should not leave the meeting, without its consent, until it concludes.

The representatives to the Yearly Meeting are to meet at the rise of its first sitting, select and nominate to its next, Friends for Clerk and Assistant, who should be separately considered, and, if approved, appointed to those stations.

Each Quarterly, Monthly, and Preparative Meeting should appoint a committee, annually, to propose Friends for Clerk, and assistant, if needed, who should be separately considered, and, if approved, appointed to those services.

The Yearly, Quarterly, and Monthly Meetings should each appoint a Treasurer, with whom annual settlements should be made.

Every Monthly Meeting, once in three years, or oftener if necessary, is to appoint a Friend to keep a record of certificates of marriage and certificates of removal as issued and received; also a Friend to record births and deaths of members, and *all* burials in our grounds, as well as the places of interment of members elsewhere, on receipt of an account of the same from the committee appointed to collect them.

These records should be made in suitable books provided by the Monthly Meeting.

When a Yearly, Quarterly, or Monthly Meeting shall request of those subordinate to it a copy of their proceedings in any case, the latter should readily comply, and make such corrections as the superior meeting may direct.

Quarterly and Monthly Meetings, when requested, should give to co-ordinate meetings copies of such of their records as may concern them; and may, at their discretion, give to their members who have had differences, copies of minutes relative thereto.

No Quarterly Meeting is to be set up or discontinued but by the Yearly Meeting; no Monthly Meeting but by the Quarterly; and no Preparative, or meeting for worship, but by the Monthly, with the approbation of the

Quarterly Meeting. Should a proposed new meeting be of members from more than one Monthly Meeting, they, and the meetings to which they are subordinate, should in like manner participate, and, if established, a few concerned Friends should be deputed by each Monthly Meeting to attend the opening thereof and designate the meeting to which it shall be subordinate. The setting up or laying down of any meeting should be reported to the next Yearly Meeting.

All certificates, minutes, or other writings issued by authority of any meeting should be signed by the Clerk or Clerks on behalf thereof; and each meeting, except the Preparative, should keep a permanent record of its proceedings.

The Clerk of a meeting should forward its reports to the Clerk of its superior meeting before the opening of the same, that time may be saved by a suitable arrangement of the business to come before it.

A Monthly Meeting may apply to the Quarterly Meeting for assistance in difficult cases; or, if the circumstances require, refer them by minute thereto. In a case involving the right to appeal, the Monthly Meeting should inform the Quarterly that a subject is before it in which it desires assistance; whereupon the latter should appoint a committee to sit with and assist the former and report its attendance, no allusion being made to the merits of the case either in the application or the report.

QUERIES.

That superior meetings may be clearly informed of the condition of society, and that Friends may be led to an individual examination as to whether their practice is consistent with their profession, and that ministers, elders, overseers, and other religiously concerned Friends may be incited to a faithful discharge of their duty in administering counsel and admonition, it is directed that the following Queries be read in the Preparative and Monthly Meetings (in the latter only if the members of both be the same), deliberately considered, and answered in their reports to the Quarterly Meeting which next precedes the Yearly Meeting, to which it is to forward summaries; also, that the first six Queries be read in like manner, and explicit answers thereto reported to all the Quarterly Meetings, in which summaries shall be made and recorded:

First Query. Are Friends diligent and punctual in the attendance of meetings for worship and discipline, and careful to maintain devotional solemnity therein? Have any meetings been omitted?

Second. Are love and unity maintained, and if differences arise is due care taken to end them? Do Friends strive so to live as to be a good example to all?

Third. When members violate any of our

testimonies, is due watchfulness observed to extend to them Christian care for their restoration?

Fourth. Are Friends careful to observe moderation, simplicity, and plainness, and do they endeavor to train their children, and those under their care, in a life and conversation consistent with our Christian profession?

Fifth. Do Friends encourage the reading of the Scriptures, and meditation thereon, and by their attendance and advice endeavor to promote the interest of First-day schools? Is care taken to give instruction in our principles and testimonies?

Sixth. Are Friends clear of giving aid in any way to the manufacture, sale, and use of intoxicating liquors as a beverage or in the preparation of food, and are they diligent in discouraging the same? Do they avoid places where such liquors are sold, and all places of a demoralizing tendency? Is the cultivation and use of tobacco, and the use of all other narcotics, discouraged?

Seventh. Have the records of births, deaths and burials been made and reported to the Monthly Meeting? Are our burial grounds kept in good order?

Eighth. Are the circumstances of members who require aid inspected, and is relief afforded? Are they advised and assisted in suitable employments? Is care taken to promote the school education of their children?

Ninth. Do Friends encourage a free gospel ministry, resting upon Divine qualification?

Tenth. Do Friends encourage arbitration as opposed to war, and do they avoid and discourage oaths, and all forms of lotteries, gambling, bribery and oppression?

Eleventh. Are Friends careful to live within their means, and do they conduct their business in a manner becoming their religious profession, and avoid extending it beyond their ability to manage? Where any give reasonable grounds for fear in these respects, is care extended to them?

Twelfth. Are the queries, including the introductory paragraphs, and "The Advices" read in the subordinate meetings, and are the former answered therein as directed?

ADVICES.

It is further directed that the following advices be read, at least once a year, in the subordinate meetings, with a suitable pause between them, as a means of awakening in those present a consideration whether there is any occasion for an extension of care in these respects, in relation either to themselves or others.

FRIENDS ARE ADVISED: To observe moderation in furnishing their homes, and in their manner of living.

To encourage their fellow-beings in abstaining from the use of everything hurtful.

To attend to the limitations of truth in their

temporal business, inspect the state of their worldly affairs once in a year, and make their wills while in health.

To apply for certificates when about to remove, and to pay proper attention to those coming from other places, who appear as Friends without producing certificates; to be careful to extend cordial welcome to young people and strangers who attend our meetings.

When any give occasion for uneasiness, to speak to them in privacy and with tenderness before the matter be communicated to another. Then, should further exercise of the Discipline be necessary, those intrusted with it will not be weakened by a consciousness that the true order of the Gospel, as explained in Matt. 18: 15, 16 and 17, has been violated.

Friends are earnestly advised to read and study the Discipline, that they may learn to realize and appreciate the wisdom and beauty of the system it is intended to uphold.

MINISTRY.

Friends have always believed that it is only under the immediate teaching and influence of the Holy Spirit that acceptable worship is performed and a pure gospel ministry supplied, and that this pure and powerful influence is the essential qualification for the work. They also believe the giving and receiving of a stated salary as a minister to be contrary to the spirit and freedom of the Gospel, tending to make merchandise of it, and therefore dangerous to the cause of true righteousness, and a hindrance to the faithful minister, by being a great temptation to such as are not thoroughly grounded in Christ the Spiritual Son and power of God in the soul.

While Friends consider the gift of the ministry to be of so pure and sacred a nature that no payment should be made or accepted for its exercise, and that it ought never be undertaken for a pecuniary consideration, yet they do not question the propriety of supplying means, when necessary, for the performance of any Gospel service. Believing that this gift of the Holy Spirit comes from God only, ministry ought not to be demanded at stated times, but it should be exercised in the ability which God gives on the occasion. Ministers should be careful to act in accordance with this distinct principle, as presented in the example of the Apostles and other early teachers of Christianity, and particularly by Jesus Christ, the beloved son of God.

While recognizing the fact that the unlettered are often qualified to be true and powerful ministers of the Gospel, yet, as all ability is useful when under right direction, it is desired that all should properly cultivate the talents God has given them, that their labor may be broader and more useful by being clothed in the language and conceptions of a well developed mind kept under the guidance of the Spirit of Truth. When under this guidance Friends are cautioned not to withhold that which they feel called upon to speak, as such a course will "tend to poverty."

MINISTERS.

When a Friend has frequently appeared in public testimony, and the Preparative Meeting of Ministers and Elders agrees in proposing that he be recommended as a minister, it is to inform the Quarterly Meeting of Ministers and Elders thereof, and if the latter concur, the former should propose the consideration of the subject to the Monthly Meeting, and if it should approve the ministry of the Friend, he shall then be recognized as an approved minister, and the Monthly Meeting is to inform the Preparative, and it the Quarterly Meeting of Ministers and Elders thereof.

No Friend is to travel abroad as a minister, or appoint meetings, unless previously approved by the Monthly Meeting.

When a minister feels it to be his religious duty to travel in the ministry within the limits of the Quarterly Meeting to which he belongs, the approbation of the Monthly Meeting should be obtained, except in appointing a few meetings near home, when the approbation of the ministers and elders will be sufficient. If the duty be to travel in other parts of the Yearly Meeting, a certificate of unity is to be procured, unless the visit be to a neighboring Quarterly Meeting and the Monthly Meeting should judge it unnecessary.

If the concern be to make an extensive visit among those not of our society, or a general visit in another Yearly Meeting, the concurrence of the Quarterly Meeting is to be obtained and endorsed on the certificate of the Monthly Meeting.

When a minister has a concern to make a religious visit to foreign countries, the clearest evidence should be obtained of the propriety of the undertaking, and the approval of the Yearly Meeting also should be secured and endorsed on the certificate previously obtained.

As the performance of religious visits to

families, under the right direction, has proved useful and instructive, it is hoped ministers will not be unfaithful to any intimation of duty in that direction. It is desired that those who are favored with such a mission, even in the Monthly Meeting to which they belong, should have the concurrence of that meeting. A certificate of unity should be obtained if the concern extend to the families of another Monthly Meeting.

When ministers remote from home, on appointments of the Yearly Meeting, have a concern to appoint meetings, they should obtain the approbation of such Friends as may be convenient before proceeding therein.

When certificates are granted to ministers, the limits of the concern should be expressed, and they should be seasonably returned. It is also expected that strangers who are with us as ministers will have certificates of unity, which, if not presented, should be inquired for.

When any certificate of unity is presented and read, a minute thereof should be made.

ELDERS.

Monthly Meetings once in three years, or oftener if necessary, are to appoint a committee of men and women to propose two or more Friends to fill the position of Elders. Those named should be separately considered at the next subsequent meeting, and, if approved, they are to become members of the Meetings for Ministers and Elders, information of which should be given to the Preparative Meeting of that body, which is to record the names and notify their Quarterly, which is to give the information to their Yearly Meeting. These triennial appointments are to be considered as a release to those who have filled that position, unless reappointed.

When an Elder removes from one Monthly Meeting to another his appointment ceases.

MEETINGS FOR MINISTERS AND ELDERS.

The Ministers and Elders of a Monthly Meeting, or of more than one if the Quarterly Meeting for Discipline advise it, are to meet once in three months and compose a Preparative Meeting of Ministers and Elders. The members of all such within the verge of a Quarterly Meeting for Discipline, are to meet once in three months and constitute a Quarterly Meeting of Ministers and Elders, and the members of all such Quarterly Meetings are to meet annually, and compose a Yearly Meeting of Ministers and Elders. The particular times and places of holding these meetings are subject to the direction of the Meetings for Discipline, to which they are severally attached. They are not to interfere with the disciplinary affairs of the Society.

As much depends on the labors and example of ministers and elders, these meetings have been established among them for the purpose of examining whether they are all preserved in an exemplary life corresponding with their position; where advice and caution may be administered for the help and strength one of another; and with this view, the following queries are to be read and answered in them.

First. By each of their Preparative Meetings, which shall give explicit answers thereto in writing, and forward them to the Quarterly Meeting.

Second. By each of their Quarterly Meetings in connection with the answers from the subordinate meetings, of which summaries should be minuted; and those made at the meeting next preceding their annual gathering should be included in its reports thereto.

Third. By their Yearly Meeting, in connection with the answers from their Quarterly Meetings, summaries whereof should be made and recorded.

The Clerk of each meeting should forward its reports to the Clerk of its superior meeting.

QUERIES FOR MINISTERS AND ELDERS.

First query. Are ministers and elders diligent and punctual in the attendance of meetings for worship and discipline, and concerned to encourage their families in that religious duty?

Second. Are ministers careful to minister in the ability which Truth gives, to avoid unbecoming tones and gestures, and prolonging their testimony so as to be burdensome?

Third. Are ministers and elders in unity one with another and with the meetings to which they belong; and do they manifest a religious concern for the advancement of Truth and the exercise of our discipline?

Fourth. Are elders careful to encourage judiciously all who appear to have a gift in the ministry? Do they counsel and admonish those whose communications appear hurtful?

Fifth. Are ministers and elders good examples in uprightness and moderation; and are they careful to instruct their families in the principles and testimonies of our religious Society?

ADVICE TO MINISTERS AND ELDERS.

It is desired that the following advices also be deliberately read in each of their subordinate meetings:

Ministers should be cautious not to use unnecessary preambles in their testimonies, nor assert too positively a Divine impulse, the baptizing power of Truth accompanying their words being the true evidence.

The Holy Scriptures should be frequently read, and care taken not to misquote nor misapply them.

Ministers should be careful how they speak upon disputed points in their testimony, or make statements which they can not clearly sustain.

The solemnity of meetings should not be disturbed by unnecessary additions towards their conclusion.

As the Author of all good continues from time to time to open among us the spring of living ministry, it is fervently desired that ministers and elders may so dwell under the Divine influence as to be enabled to discern when offerings proceed from the source of Life and Light, being thus qualified to instruct and encourage those who are young in the ministry with gentleness and wisdom, advising and encouraging them to abide in simple and patient submission to the will of God, and keep to the openings of Divine life in themselves, by which they will experience a growth in their gifts.

All are especially cautioned against any harshness or severity of tone or manner when administering counsel or reproof, remembering that they who would do the Father's work must "abide in His love." Even a *seeming* harshness may check the beginning of true repentance, and lack of sympathy cause a blight to fall where only good was intended.

Should ministers and elders, by unfaithfulness or other cause, lose their usefulness, a timely and tender care should be extended by individuals, and, if necessary, by the Preparative or Quarterly Meeting of Ministers and Elders of which they are members, and if the desired effect is not produced, such cases should be laid before the Monthly Meeting for such action as it may deem proper.

If a meeting should be disturbed by improper communications the ministers and elders should extend advice and counsel as may seem necessary, and if such admonition be ineffectual, the case should be laid before the Preparative Meeting for Ministers and Elders, and if the further care of this Meeting be unavailing, it should lay the case before the Monthly Meeting, which is to treat with the offender as may appear necessary.

And, lastly, let all dwell in that spirit which gives ability to labor successfully in the Church of Christ, adorning the doctrine they deliver to others by being examples in word, in conversation, in charity, in spirit, in faith and in purity.

The Meetings for Ministers and Elders are intended for their members only, but ministers and their companions, or elders from other Meetings may sit in them, and any Friend may do so by request, if no objection be made.

Preparative Meetings of Ministers and Elders should annually make a report to their respective Monthly Meetings for Discipline, of such of their proceedings as will, in their judgment, be of profit and interest to that body.

PROPERTY AND FUNDS.

All our Meetings are directed to make timely and careful inspection into the situation of the titles to their lands, burial grounds, and other estates which have been vested in them or in trustees for their use and benefit; and upon the death or removal of any such trustee, seasonably to appoint another to the trust.

It is further directed that all our Meetings be careful to have duly recorded and preserve their title papers, keep a record of the appointment of their trustees, the place where, and with whom their papers, minutes and records are deposited, due care being taken to lodge them with suitable persons.

A Yearly Meeting fund having, by experience, been found necessary for the exigencies of the Society, it is directed that such a fund be maintained by an occasional collection from each Quarterly Meeting, in the proportion which may from time to time be determined by the Yearly Meeting, and that it be placed in the hands of a treasurer appointed by the Meeting, subject to be drawn out by its direction.

Quarterly and Monthly Meetings are also directed to keep a fund, to be used for such purposes as their respective wants may render necessary. Such funds, and those for the use of the Yearly Meeting, are to be raised by voluntary contributions.

Women's Meetings should also have a fund, raised in like manner, for use in such services as may come specially under their notice and care.

OVERSEERS.

Monthly Meetings should appoint, every three years or oftener, for themselves, or for each of their Preparative Meetings, where such exist, two or more members of each sex to serve as Overseers. They should be nominated by a joint committee of men and women, and the Friends proposed be separately considered by the Meeting one month after they are reported, and if approved, appointed.

Overseers are to act jointly in considering applications for membership, and in all other cases when expedient.

They should be familiar with the discipline, and endeavor to exercise Christian care over their fellow members, and if any manifestations hurtful to right principles, or contrary to harmony and good order appear, give seasonable attention thereto.

TREATMENT FOR DEVIATIONS.

As the purpose of our labor in every case of deviation is the restoration to sound principles, upright life, and true fellowship of those who have departed therefrom, they should be treated with in a Christian spirit, patiently and prayerfully, and all right opportunities used to accomplish this end; and while diligent, overseers and committees should avoid pressing any case to an unfavorable conclusion while reasonable hope of restoration remains.

Even if those who transgress should manifest a spirit of opposition, we ought, patiently and meekly, to instruct and advise them, that we may not only have the reward of peace in ourselves, but that it may so affect the spirit of those spoken to as to make them realize that we have performed a Christian duty and an office of brotherly love towards them.

If the endeavors of overseers, or other concerned Friends, to restore any who have violated the principles or good order of the Society are unavailing, the former should report the case to the Monthly or Preparative Meeting without unnecessary delay, notice having been previously given to the person complained of, who should not attend the meetings for discipline until the case is disposed of.

Monthly Meetings, upon presentation of a complaint against a member, should enter it upon the minutes, and appoint a committee to extend further care in the case, that reconciliation may be effected if possible. This committee should give seasonable attention to its appointment.

When a satisfactory acknowledgment has been received from one who has deviated, a committee should be appointed to so inform him. If, having failed to reclaim, the Monthly Meeting thinks it right to cancel the membership, it should appoint a committee to inform him of the judgment of the meeting, furnish him with a copy of the complaint, if required, and notify him of his privilege of appealing, and endeavor to leave him in a tender frame of mind, and convince him that it is only his own departure from our principles and profession that is the cause of his separation from the Society, and that we earnestly desire that he may be convinced of the error of his ways.

When a member residing within the verge of a Monthly Meeting to which his right has not been transferred, deviates from our order, he should be visited by the overseers, who, if necessary, should inform the overseers of the meeting to which he belongs of such deviation.

If any member speak in an irreverent spirit of the Scriptures or of sacred matters therein contained, he should be treated with.

APPEALS.

If a person be dissatisfied with the judgment of a Monthly Meeting in his case, he may, after being informed thereof, notify the first or second meeting thereafter of his intention to appeal to the next Quarterly Meeting, which notification the Monthly Meeting should record, and appoint two or more Friends to attend the Quarterly Meeting with copies of the minutes relative to the case, to give such explanations as may be necessary.

The Quarterly Meeting is to refer the subject to a committee (omitting the members of the Meeting appealed from), which is to examine the whole proceedings in the case, giving the appellant and the Monthly Meeting's committee a full hearing; if it finds the charge substantiated and the proceedings in accordance with our Discipline, it is to so report; the Quarterly Meeting is thereupon to confirm the judgment of the Monthly Meeting, and inform said Meeting and the appellant of the result. But, if it appear that the deviation, or the proof thereof is not sufficient, or there has been irregularity in the proceedings infringing the rights of the appellant, it is to report accordingly, and the judgment of the Monthly Meeting should be set aside. If the grounds of such reversal be irregularity of proceeding only, the Monthly Meeting shall be at liberty to take up the case again.

Should the appellant be dissatisfied with the

decision of the Quarterly Meeting, he may notify its first or second meeting next succeeding such information of his intention to apply to the Yearly Meeting for a further hearing. The notice should be recorded, and four or more Friends appointed to attend with the minutes of both the Monthly and Quarterly Meetings in the case, and the decision of the Yearly Meeting shall be final.

Appellants have a right to be present in the Meetings appealed to during the appointment of the committee to judge in their cases, and objections they may make to persons nominated are to be considered and judged of by the meeting.

Appeals should be forwarded to superior meetings in the regular reports, and the appellant, if he give opportunity, should be notified when to be present; also of the judgment of the meeting in his case.

MARRIAGE.

Marriage being a Divine ordinance affecting all the relations of life, it is of vital importance that those who propose to enter therein should humbly seek for guidance from our Heavenly Father, with a prayerful desire to be directed aright, not neglecting to counsel with their parents or guardians, and to give earnest heed to their deliberate advice, in giving which parents and guardians are entreated to seek wisdom from the Lord.

Experience has proven that the affections are not always a certain guide, and that true worth and congeniality of taste, thought, and disposition are requisite for the right formation of so solemn a compact. For this reason we would extend earnest caution against our members marrying those holding no settled religious convictions, or views opposed to our principles and testimonies, such alliances being frequently productive of unhappy results.

Marriages of persons sooner than one year after the death of husband or wife, or of those so nearly related as first cousins, or of the children of half brothers or sisters, are not to be permitted among us; nor should any of our members avail themselves of legal privileges to dissolve the marriage contract. If any do, they should be treated with as for other deviations.

For the accomplishing of marriage, the following order is recommended to be observed:

The parties are to communicate their intentions to the Monthly Meeting, under the care of which the marriage is to take place, in a written statement signed by both, in substance as follows:

To ―― Monthly Meeting of Friends:

We intend marriage with each other, and desire to accomplish the same under the care of the meeting.

[Signed] ―――― ――――
 ―――― ――――

Whereupon, if they belong to the same meeting, a committee of men and women Friends should be appointed to extend necessary care. If they have parents or guardians, their consent, when it can reasonably be obtained, should be given to the meeting in writing. Should either party have children, the committee is to see that their rights are legally secured.

At the next meeting, if the committee reports that no obstruction to the further proceeding appears, the Monthly Meeting may leave the parties at liberty to accomplish their marriage according to our order, at a public meeting, or at such time and place as it may approve, but not on the first day of the week. Two Friends of each sex (whose names may be proposed by the parties, subject to the approval of the meeting) are to be appointed to attend the marriage, have a care that good order be observed, and see that the certificate be recorded.

If either be a member of another Monthly

Meeting, a certificate should be presented therefrom, showing that no obstruction appears. Misdemeanors long past should not, at such times, be held by the meeting to be an objection to marriage.

The above care and sanction may also be extended in cases where one of the parties is not a member.

Friends believe that no human power can unite two persons in marriage, the solemn declarations of the parties themselves being the true marriage ceremony. Therefore we believe that a sincere obligation to the following effect, made in the presence of witnesses, is most pleasing in the sight of the Lord, as well as most satisfactory to the parties themselves, when rightly understood and appreciated.

After joining hands, they should proceed in substance as follows, he speaking first:

"In the presence of the Lord, and before these witnesses, I take thee ——— to be my wife (or husband), promising, with Divine assistance, to be unto thee a loving and faithful husband (or wife) until death shall separate us."

After these declarations, the marriage certificate should be signed by the parties and audibly read by some suitable person selected by them, or named by the committee appointed to attend the marriage. The committee should also examine the certificate previously to its being read and signed, and, if necessary, correct it.

The form of the certificate should be as follows:

Whereas, A. B., of ——, in the county of ——, and State of ——, son of C. and D. B., of ——, and D. E., daughter of F. and G. E., of ——, having informed —— Monthly Meeting of the religious Society of Friends, held at ——, that they intend marriage with each other [and, if it can be reasonably obtained, add], and having consent of parents (or guardians, as the case may be), their proposals were approved by the meeting.

These are to certify to whom it may concern,

that for the accomplishment of their marriage, this ——— day of the ——— month, in the year of our Lord ———, they, the said A. B. and D. E. appeared at ———, and in the presence of a committee appointed by the meeting; *and A. B. taking D. E. by the hand, declared that he took her to be his wife, promising, with Divine assistance, to be unto her a loving and faithful husband until death should separate them; and then D. E. did, in like manner, declare that she took him to be her husband, promising, with Divine assistance, to be unto him a loving and faithful wife until death should separate them.*

And they (she according to the custom of marriage assuming the surname of her husband) did, as a further confirmation thereof, then and there, to these presents set their hands.

A. B———.
D. E———.

And we, being present, have subscribed our names as witnesses thereof.

If for any reason the above order is not carried out, and the marriage is accomplished without seeking the approbation of the meeting, the same solemn declaration should be made by the parties, in the presence of a minister of our Society, or of a civil officer, who shall sign the marriage certificate and certify the marriage as required by law. The certificate should be handed to the Recorder.

In all cases where a license is obtained, it is desirable that it be procured and published thirty days before the marriage is to take place.

If a member should contract and effect his marriage without applying to the Monthly Meeting, he should be visited by the Overseers, and if a desire to retain his membership be evinced, and no departure from our order exists, no further action should be taken.

When no application is made by members to the Monthly Meeting, and the parties marry by the ceremony herein prescribed, the certificate should be altered accordingly, only that part in italics being used, to which should be added the names of the parents of both parties and their residence.

The marriage of a woman Friend, not accomplished under the care of the Monthly Meeting, should be recorded, together with her residence, and the names of her husband and his parents.

The violations of our testimony in the important matter of engagement and marriage being, we fear, often for want of due care on the part of parents, and others who have charge of educating the youth, in *timely* admonishing and instructing them in the principles of Truth, and impressing their minds with the duty of religiously observing them, Friends are earnestly exhorted to increase their care in this direction, guarding the associations of the young, leading them to select for companionship those who are worthy of regard and respect, and teaching them to uphold our principles and testimonies because *they* believe them to be true, being careful to show them wherein our testimony in favor of a free Gospel Ministry may be violated. It is directed that on the marriage occasions, Friends be thoughtful to set a becoming example of moderation.

PARENTS AND CHILDREN.

Parents and heads of families are entreated to lay to heart the great and lasting importance of educating the youth in righteousness, and to be solicitous that their tender and susceptible minds may be impressed with virtuous principles and a just sense of the Divine Being, His wisdom, goodness, power, and omnipresence.

The importance of an early instruction in the law of God is set forth with peculiar strength, clearness, and solemnity in Deuteronomy, VI., 4: "Hear, O Israel; the Lord our God is one Lord; and thou shalt love the Lord thy God with all thine heart, and with all thy soul, and with all thy might, and these words which I command thee this day shall be upon thine heart; and thou shalt teach them diligently unto thy children, and shalt talk of them when thou sittest in thine house, and when thou walkest by the way, and when thou liest down, and when thou risest up."

Although virtue does not descend by lineal succession, nor piety by inheritance, temperaments do, and we therefore urge upon parents to guard and restrain with great care their own tendencies to whatever is evil or excessive in their nature, and to foster whatever is good, not only as a duty to themselves, but as a help to their offspring, who will inherit their parents' temperaments in a greater or less degree.

Parents should be good examples to their children in their meetings, in their families, and in their employments. As children are given to their care, they should be faithful in watching over them, *from infancy*, for their moral growth, moulding their character in gentleness and wisdom, remembering their proper craving after things suited to their ages. They should endeavor to inculcate sound principles, and lead the children to the self-application of these principles to their daily needs, rather than to furnish them conclusions resting on the wisdom of another. It is especially desired that they be taught the propriety of restraint from reading any publications of a nature to undermine their moral character, weaken their sense of righteous duty, or alienate them from their allegiance unto God, as well as from unprofitable and demoralizing conversation. Their need for that which is instructive and cheerful should be supplied, and they should be taught the nobility and beauty as well as the duty of right doing. Let parents endeavor to educate their children in a reverent respect for goodness, purity and virtue, and thus may they be twice blessed in their efforts, once in their own lives, and again in the lives of their children.

In much love to the rising generation they are exhorted to turn away from and not yield to the many vanities and ensnaring corruptions prevalent in the world, and bear in mind that "the fear of the Lord is the beginning of wisdom." Take the advice of religiously concerned parents, guardians and friends, ever remembering that children ought to obey their parents in the Lord, and that disobedience herein is a violation of the moral law, and offensive in Divine sight.

FIRST-DAY SCHOOLS.

The Society of Friends, recognizing the value of First-day Schools in promoting an increase of interest in their spiritual welfare as individuals, and the growth and extension of the principles of truth in general, all are earnestly advised to attend and advance their usefulness as way is opened for them to do so, and to endeavor to gather the children into them, that good seeds may be implanted in their tender minds while the soil is fresh and pure. We are never too old to learn concerning the deep things of the Spirit, hence we are entrusted with the duty of helping one another by frequently assembling for the purpose of considering the truths contained in the Holy Scriptures and other writings calculated to elevate the human family in morality and righteousness. Thus, with the blessing of God upon our efforts, we will learn the beauty of a life of holiness, and encourage each other to greater faithfulness and usefulness in the Master's service.

EDUCATION.

As knowledge gives increased qualification for usefulness, it becomes us to encourage a thorough education for all, and to provide for the instruction of our children and those under our care, in whatever is useful and within the limit of their capacity and our ability. As children need moral as well as intellectual education, and are very much influenced in this respect by their surroundings during the impressible period of youth when their characters are being formed, great care should be observed to see that these are helpful and good. So far as practicable it is desirable they should attend schools under the care of teachers holding views consistent with our testimonies, and who are concerned for their right presentation to their pupils.

Friends should use their influence in securing the employment of teachers in our public schools, whose precepts and example shall lead their pupils to see the nobility and beauty of an exemplary and upright life.

SPEECH, DEPORTMENT AND APPAREL.

As our general appearance in these matters is largely indicative of the condition of our minds, and in proportion as it conforms to our profession, is more or less beneficial to ourselves and society, it is desired that members should be thoughtful in regard to the use of plain, kind, and honest words in their speech, avoiding extravagant phrases and formal compliments. All profanity, immoral and impure conversation should be strictly avoided. When our minds are regulated by the spirit and purpose of the Gospel taught by Jesus, we believe our speech will reflect with plainness and simplicity, the kindness, courtesy, justice and Christian regard that lie back of it, in the soul thus taught.

Our deportment should at all times be consistent with our profession. We should be serious and reverent in times of worship or solemnity, calm and just during our dealings or in controversy, willing and anxious to see the right on all sides. Cheerful, kind and patient in the family and social relations, thoughtful of the different temperaments of individuals and differing ages, we should upon all occasions avoid hurtful conduct and maintain true dignity.

In dress, simplicity and utility should be observed as the essentials, neatness and good taste cultivated, and extravagance and foolish fashions avoided as being promoters of pride and vanity, giving evidence of minds drawn aside from thoughts worthy of an intelligent pure-minded man or woman.

As we believe all to be equal in the sight of God, we neither give titles nor pay homage to any.

DEFAMATION AND DETRACTION.

Friends should endeavor to so keep themselves under the perfect law of love that they will neither think, nor speak, evil one of another. They should avoid all criticism of the conduct of others that may tend to produce ill feeling, as well as conversation detrimental to the character of any person, or in the nature of idle gossip. They should not only avoid giving needless circulation to evil reports concerning any one, but aid in suppressing them.

When any are guilty of tale-bearing or speaking evil of others, or meddling with their affairs when not concerned, tending to excite strife and disorder, or cause dissension among Friends or others, they are to be treated with.

MODERATION AND TEMPERANCE.

Friends are affectionately advised to be moderate in all their movements, and temperate in the use of all things necessary to sustain and comfort the body. In view of the desolating effects of the improper use of intoxicating liquors, they are earnestly entreated to avoid and discourage their manufacture, or furnishing materials therefor, and the importation, selling or use of them as a beverage. They are not permitted to use or rent their property for such purposes, and are advised not to frequent places where liquors are sold, or other places of public resort where they may be exposed to unprofitable company and conversation, and drawn into improper habits.

TOBACCO.

In view of the great waste, both physical and pecuniary, and the many other objections applicable to its use, Friends are urged seriously to ask themselves if they can properly use tobacco in any form. They are, in the love of human good, earnestly advised not to use, grow or deal in it.

CIVIL GOVERNMENT.

Friends have ever maintained that it is their duty to obey all the requirements of civil government, except those by which their allegiance to God is interfered with.

They should patiently submit in the spirit of meekness to any suffering that may befall them for non-compliance with any requisition repugnant to their principles. Let them give no just occasion for offense to those in authority, but conduct themselves circumspectly towards all men.

Liberty of conscience being the common right of all, and particularly essential to the well-being of religious societies, they hold it to be incumbent upon them to maintain it inviolably among themselves, and therefore exhort all in profession with them to decline to accept any office or station in civil government, the duties of which are inconsistent with their religious principles, or in the exercise of which, they may be or apprehend themselves to be under the necessity of exacting from others, any compliance against which they are themselves personally conscientious.

BUSINESS RELATIONS.

Unless the love of justice, mercy and truth be manifest in our dealings, we can have no claim to religion. Honesty and integrity are required of all. Friends are therefore earnestly advised not to make haste to become rich, and to avoid all hazardous enterprises, especially when the means of others may be involved, and to choose no occupation that may bring reproach upon any of our testimonies, but to select vocations that are useful, and be diligent therein. They should keep accurate accounts, inspecting them often, that they may know whether they are living within their means, thus reserving to themselves the ability to be not only just to all but kind to the unfortunate, remembering the injunction of the Golden Rule, "Therefore, all things whatsoever ye would that men should do unto you, do ye even so to them." (Mat. VII. 12.)

Friends should exercise great caution about borrowing money, or endorsing for others. While there are cases in which it may be prudent and proper, Friends entering into business are advised to seek sound advice before borrowing.

If any have doubts of their ability to fulfill their engagements or pay their just debts, they should immediately consult some judicious Friends, and, if they advise it, make a full exhibit to their creditors of their assets and liabilities, and as they direct, make settlement by assignment or otherwise without partiality. Friends are not to avoid the payment of their just debts by any legal privileges, but to make *pro rata* payments thereon as they become able.

If any member neglects the above admonitions in regard to his business pursuits, or gives rise to fear that he is doing so, he should be counseled promptly, and if his conduct continues at variance with our rules or reproachful to society, prompt and judicious care should be extended to him.

Friends are advised to be careful not to receive collections or donations from such as have refused, or have not the means, to pay their just debts.

ARBITRATION.

When difficulties arise between members of the society about their temporal concerns, the party thinking he has reason for complaint is to speak to the other in a calm and friendly manner, endeavoring by gentle means to obtain justice. If this prove ineffectual, he should take one or more of the overseers or other judicious Friends to join him in endeavors to have the matter justly and speedily settled; or if the distance between the parties be too great, the complainant should pursue the same friendly course by writing to the other, and failing in that he should empower some Friend to pursue the course above indicated on his behalf. Should the case appear to be a plain one, or a debt against which no reasonable objection is made by the debtor, the Friends are to advise the party complained of to make satisfaction without delay. Should unsettled differences in accounts or other cause for dispute appear which cannot be settled between the parties themselves, they are to advise them to submit the case to arbitration. If either party refuse to do this, such refusal is to be reported to the Preparative, and, if necessary, to the Monthly Meeting in which the proceedings in the case are to be reviewed, and if the above Gospel order has not been observed, the case should be referred back to the Preparative Meeting without being minuted; but if the proceedings in the case are approved, the meeting should appoint a committee to confer with the parties, and report the result thereof, when, if it appear necessary, the parties should be again advised to submit to arbitration, and if either of them refuse to comply, the right of membership of the person so refusing should be canceled.

When parties conclude to submit their differences to arbitration they are each to name one Friend, the two so chosen to select a third, and enter into a written agreement to abide by their decision. The arbitrators chosen should promptly appoint a time and place, and attend to the business without unnecessary delay, giving the parties and their witnesses a full and fair hearing in the presence of each other, and endeavor to make the award promptly.

If either of the parties be dissatisfied with the award, and it be very evident that the arbitrators have erred materially in their proceedings or judgment, the Monthly may apply to the Quarterly Meeting for assistance, as directed in difficult cases, and should it clearly appear there is cause for dissatisfaction, a rehearing is to be granted and other arbitrators chosen, whose decision shall be final.

It is advised that Friends in the ministry be not chosen as arbitrators in any case.

When the foregoing proceedings, by causing delay, would evidently endanger the rights of the complainant, or subject him to loss which might be avoided by a more direct legal process, Monthly Meetings may hold such excused as apply to the law from such necessity; but they are cautioned to conduct themselves toward each other with such kindness and moderation as will be a becoming testimony, even in court, that only the nature of the case and our station under the laws of the land bring any of us there.

If any member sue another at law, or cause his arrest in disregard of the foregoing rules, he should be dealt with as for other deviations.

Meetings for discipline should not take part in controversies between members and non-members, except to encourage settlement by arbitration.

When arbitrators are at a loss for want of legal knowledge it will be proper for them, at the joint expense of the parties, to take the opinion of counsel learned in the law to enable them to give a proper judgment in the matters referred to them. That they may better answer the end of their appointment, and be helpful in conciliating the minds of the parties, they ought not to consider themselves as advocates for those by whom they are chosen, but as men whose duty it is to judge righteously. They should shun all previous information respecting the case, or, having heard anything in regard to it, remain as much as possible unbiased thereby. They should not refuse to hear any evidence that may be offered, nor receive any except in the presence of both parties, and in their award they need not assign any reason for their determination

WAR.

Believing that the spirit of the Gospel breathes "on earth peace among men," it is the earnest concern of Friends that they may adhere faithfully to their testimony against war. As pertinent to the subject, it is further earnestly enjoined upon all Friends to actively give their aid and encouragement to measures that have for their object the promotion of peace and the settlement of difficulties by arbitration, both those of a national and international character.

OATHS.

As a judicial oath rests upon the principle of calling a superior power to witness the truth of what is to be declared, and is an assumption that except in this presence the person would not, or might not tell the truth, and believing it to be contrary to the explicit injunction of Jesus, "Ye have heard that it was said to them of old time, 'Thou shalt not forswear thyself, but shalt perform unto the Lord thine oaths;' but I say unto you swear not at all;" to which the Apostle James adds, "Swear not, neither by the heaven nor by the earth, nor by any other oath; but let your yea be yea, and your nay, nay; that ye fall not under judgment." Friends have always felt bound to bear testimony against all oaths, and when required by law either to take or administer a legal qualification, substitute an affirmation.

OPPRESSION.

It has been and continues to be the earnest concern of the Society to bear a faithful testimony against the oppression of mankind wherever practiced, and Friends are tenderly solicited to attend to the requirements of truth and justice in this respect, and especially to use their influence against unjust legislation.

INDIANS AND THE AFRICAN RACE.

Ever since the settlement of Friends in America the aborigines have received our earnest and continued efforts for just treatment and improvement, and Friends are affectionately entreated to continue these efforts.

It is worthy of serious consideration whether there is any object of beneficence more deserving of attention than the improvement of the condition of those of the African race who have been held in slavery and their descendants, and of the Indians of our country, and the moral and intellectual education of the children of those races, so as to make them useful and respectable members of the community.

GAMING AND PLACES OF DIVERSION.

Believing that wagering, or giving or receiving value without exchanging an equivalent, is wrong in principle and destructive in practice, Friends bear a testimony against lotteries, prize packages, betting, gambling, etc., and when any Friend departs so far from the principles of honesty and right as to participate in any of these things, early and earnest efforts should be made to convince him of his error.

Parents and concerned Friends should earnestly discourage, by precept and example, the attendance of their children and others at places of unprofitable amusement, especially such as are calculated to teach false ideas of life and duty, or to bring them into hurtful associations.

Amusements or diversions that cause needless suffering to any of God's creatures should not be considered harmless; neither should those that cannot be looked back to and remembered without regret or remorse. Such only should be engaged in as bring comfort and happiness by the remembrance of them.

MEMBERS WHO REQUIRE AID.

As mercy, compassion and charity are specially enjoined upon all Christians, Monthly and Preparative Meetings should appoint, every three years, Friends to inspect the circumstances of members who require aid, that advice and assistance may be seasonably extended, not only to relieve their immediate necessities, but to aid them in the education of their children and in suitable employment. Friends are advised to be liberal in raising funds for these purposes, also to be cautious in extending this benevolent care not unnecessarily to expose the names or situation of the recipients thereof. Those receiving should also manifest a becoming disposition to accept, and conform to the counsel of their friends. Should there be an unwillingness to conform to advice, committees are to be governed in the distribution of the intended liberality by prudence and discretion.

Those needing relief should not hesitate, but should promptly make their necessities known to this committee.

WILLS.

Friends are advised to make their wills in time of health, to renew them as often as occasion may require, and to dispose of their property according to the requirements of justice, laying aside all resentments, lest wrong may be done. They should, as a matter of prudence, consult some of their judicious friends as to the disposition of their estates.

As much depends on executors and guardians in the confidential trusts committed to them, not only in reference to the care and disposition of property, but also as to the education and welfare of minor children, Friends should exercise sound discretion in choosing them.

Those employed to draft wills should be of good judgment in such matters, and have competent legal knowledge both of the subject and of language to express it clearly. Wills should empower the executors to submit all matters in dispute relative to the estate, to arbitration.

Friends are advised, if they propose to make a donation for any charitable, benevolent or other public purpose, to do so during life, that their intentions may be carried out as they desire.

DEATHS AND BURIALS.

Monthly Meetings are annually to appoint a committee, of whom one or more should be from each Preparative Meeting (if there be more than one), to collect the accounts of deaths of its members, which accounts are to be handed promptly to the Recorder. They shall have charge of burial grounds, see that they are kept in order, and, if practicable, attend the funerals of all who are buried therein. A permit from this committee, designating the space to be occupied, is required before an interment can take place in grounds belonging to the meeting.

There should be two accurate plots, designating by number each burial space in the ground, one to be in the care of the committee, and the other to be given to the sexton regularly employed by it. They shall enter, in its proper place on their respective plots, the name of the person buried, and report promptly the name, date and number of space to the Recorder.

Friends are advised to avoid extravagance in the burial of the dead, and none should be permitted to bury in the grounds belonging to the Society who are not content with our plain and solemn order.

MEMORIALS.

The commemoration of the lives of the righteous may prove an incentive to the living to emulate their virtues. Should a Monthly Meeting, believing that it would be profitable, prepare a memorial concerning one of its deceased members, it should be sent to the Quarterly Meeting, and if approved by it, forwarded with a minute of endorsement to the Representative committee for its inspection, and correction if necessary, and if approved, forwarded to the Yearly Meeting.

The Monthly, through the Quarterly, should furnish the Yearly Meeting with the names, date of decease, and late residence of all ministers who have died within the year.

AMENDMENT OF DISCIPLINE.

All proposals for amendment or revision of Discipline shall be considered by a joint committee of men and women Friends in each meeting to which they shall be submitted, but they shall not become operative until approved and adopted by the Yearly Meeting, which shall thereupon notify those meetings subordinate to it of such amendment or revision. Said proposals may originate in any meeting for Discipline, but if in a subordinate Meeting they shall be forwarded when approved to each successive superior meeting.

APPENDIX.

Extract from the will of Alban Fawcett, deceased:

"ITEM 3. I give and devise to the Society of Friends (sometimes called Hicksites), holding their Yearly Meeting at Waynesville, Ohio, and at Richmond, Indiana, One Thousand Dollars, to be paid out of my estate, for such charitable purposes as the said Yearly meetings in their wisdom may think best."

Executed 5th Month 29, 1862. Admitted to record in Clinton county, Ohio, 6th Month 16, 1862.

Extract from the will of Jason Evans, deceased:

"ITEM 4. I give and bequeath to the Indiana Yearly Meeting of Friends that is held alternately at Richmond, Indiana, and Waynesville, Ohio, of which Aaron Wright, of Springboro, is clerk, the sum of five thousand dollars, to be placed in the hands of three trustees appointed by said Meeting, and by them invested or loaned on interest, the amount of interest or income received to be reported annually to said Yearly Meeting and by it apportioned among the Quarterly Meetings, and the said Quarterly Meetings to be instructed to apportion said amount among their respective Monthly Meetings, to be used for the benefit of the poor among their members.

"It is my desire that Friends, in making the distribution of the funds may have a due regard for the circumstances of Friends in the several meetings."

Executed 3d Month 20th, 1874. Admitted to record in Hamilton county, Ohio, 3d Month 16th, 1876.

Section 6385 Revised Statutes of Ohio:

"It shall be lawful for any ordained minister of any religious society or congregation within this State, who has or may hereafter obtain a license for that purpose, as hereinafter provided, or for any justice of the peace in his county, or for the mayor of any city or incorporated village in any county in which such city or village may wholly or partly lie, *or for the several religious societies, agreeably to the rules and regulations of their respective churches,* to join together as husband and wife all persons not prohibited by law." [April 5, 1891.]

Section 6389 Revised Statutes of Ohio:

"Previous to persons being joined in marriage, notice thereof shall be published (in the presence of the congregation), on two different days of public worship; the first publication to be at least ten days previous to such marriage, within the county where the female resides; or a license shall be obtained for that purpose from the probate judge in the county where such female may reside."

Section 6391 Revised Statutes of Ohio:

"A certificate of every marriage hereafter solemnized, whether authorized by publication of bans in the congregation or by license issued by a probate judge, or after notice given to the congregation signed by the justice, mayor or minister solemnizing the same, *or clerk of the Monthly Meeting,* shall be transmitted to the probate judge in the county wherein the marriage license was issued, or the congregation wherein said bans were published is situated, or marriage was celebrated, within three months thereafter, and recorded by said probate judge; every justice, mayor or minister, or clerk of the Monthly Meeting failing to transmit such certificate to the probate judge in due time shall forfeit and pay fifty dollars, and if the probate judge shall neglect to make such record he shall forfeit and pay fifty dollars to and for the use of the county." [April 5, 1889.]

Section 4200 Revised Statutes of Ohio:

"No estate in fee simple, fee tail, or any lesser estate, in lands or tenements, lying within this State, shall be given or granted, by deed or will, to any person or persons but such as are in being, or to the immediate issue or descendants of such as are in being at the time of making such deed or will; and all estates given in tail shall be and remain an absolute estate in fee simple to the issue of the first donee in tail."

Indiana Revised Statutes, 1881:

SECTION 5326. Marriages may be solemnized by ministers of the Gospel and priests of any church throughout the State, judges of courts of record and justices of the peace within their respective counties, and by the Society of Friends, and German Baptists, according to the rules of their societies. *Provided*, That no marriage, legal in other respects, shall be void on account of the incapacity of the person solemnizing the same."

"SEC. 5327. Before any person, except members of the Society of Friends, shall be joined in marriage they shall produce a license from the clerk of the Circuit Court of the county in which the female resides, directed to any person empowered by law to solemnize marriages, and authorizing him to join together the persons therein named as husband and wife."

"Sec. 5330. No marriage shall be void or voidable for want of license or other formality required by law, if either of the parties thereto believed it to be a legal marriage at the time."

ERRATA.

Page 37, sixth line, the words "life" and "power" should have been printed with capitals.

Page 47, third line of second query, for "so to live" read "to so live."

Page 79, third line from the last, omit the word "the."

INDEX.

	PAGE
Advices	50
Advice to Ministers and Elders	60
Aid, members requiring	101
Amendment of Discipline	106
Appeals	69
Appendix	107
Arbitration	93
Business relations	91
Cancellation of membership	29
Civil government	89
Deaths and burials	104
Defamation and detraction	87
Education	84
Elders	57
First-day schools	83
Gaming and places of diversion	100
Indians and Africans	99
Marriage	72
Membership	22
Meetings for worship	36
Meetings for Ministers and Elders	57
Meetings for Discipline	39
Memorials	105
Minors	24
Ministry	52
Ministers	54
Moderation and temperance	88

INDEX.

	PAGE
Oaths	98
Origin of Friends	12
Oppression	99
Overseers	65
Parents and children	80
Property and funds	64
Queries	46
Queries for Ministers and Elders	59
Removals and certificates	28
Representative Committee	32
Resignations	25
Register, form of	26
Speech, deportment, and apparel	85
Statistics of membership	30
Tobacco	89
Treatment for deviations	66
War	97
Wills	102
Yearly Meeting	18

www.ingramcontent.com/pod-product-compliance
Lightning Source LLC
Chambersburg PA
CBHW020148170426
43199CB00010B/940